BISON

This new edition published in 2005 by Smart Apple Media
2140 Howard Drive West, North Mankato, MN 56003
ISBN 1-58340-679-4

Design and Production by The Design Lab/Kathy Petelinsek

Photographs by Visuals Unlimited
Additional photographs by Tom Stack & Associates (pages 2, 3, 22)

The Library of Congress has cataloged the earlier edition as follows:
Library of Congress Cataloging-in-Publication Data
Wrobel, Scott.
Bison / by Scott Wrobel
p. cm. – (Northern Trek)
Includes resources, glossary, and index
Summary: Discusses the history of the American bison, commonly called the buffalo,
its physical characteristics and habits, and efforts to preserve the species.
ISBN 1-58340-031-1
1. American bison–Juvenile literature. [1. Bison.] I. Title. II. Series: Northern Trek (Mankato, Minn.)

QL737.U53W76   2000
599.64'3–dc21   98-43885

First paperback edition

2 4 6 8 9 7 5 3 1

NORTHERN TREK

BISON

WRITTEN BY SCOTT WROBEL
PHOTOGRAPHS BY VISUALS UNLIMITED

SMART APPLE MEDIA

For generations the American bison has been a symbol of the American West. Though their numbers are small today, just one hundred years ago millions of these mighty animals covered the Great Plains. Massive herds thundered across the prairie, trampling paths hundreds of yards wide. Early white settlers were often frightened by the bison. Later, the bison became a prized trophy, and settlers began hunting the animals in great numbers. Soon, the bison was nearly wiped out. Today, with the help of people who recognize the importance of bison, thousands of these animals roam throughout parks and reserves.

BISON *(Bison bison)*, also known as buffalo, are the largest mammals in North America. A full-grown male, called a bull, can stand more than six feet (1.8 m) tall at the shoulders and weigh up to 2,000 pounds (907 kg). Females, called cows, generally weigh around 1,000 pounds (455 kg). The bison's long, thick skull is covered by two inches (5 cm) of skin and a carpet of dense fur. Curved horns grow from both sides of the skull. Unlike elk and deer antlers, bison horns do not shed, or fall off and regrow.

The bison's body is especially enormous at the hump that rises up between its shoulders. The front half of its body seems too big for its **hindquarters**. This is because the shoulders, hump, and skull are covered by five times the amount of fur that covers the rest of the body. The thick fur in these regions protects the bison's **vital organs** and skin from cold weather and deep snow.

The hulking, brown-coated body of the bison is similar to that of its North American neighbor, the moose.

Bison have poor eyesight, but their other senses make up for this weakness. Their ears, located behind their horns, are capable of hearing the smallest sounds up to 300 yards (274 m) away. The bison's nose is also highly sensitive. When scents are carried on the wind, a bison can tell the difference between kinds of animals up to a mile (1.6 km) away.

When summer arrives, so do the flies. To swat bugs off their hides, bison constantly flick their tails. Bison may also create large patches of dirt by tearing up the ground with their horns. Then they fall sideways into the dirt and roll around, pressing dirt into their coats to keep the insects out. When it rains, bison roll in mud, allowing the mud

Growing from the bison's chin is one of its most unique features: a beard that can be more than 12 inches (30.5 cm) long.

Bison fur is heavy and warm, protecting the animals from enemies such as wolves and mountain lions. These predators often attack young calves that haven't yet grown thick, protective fur around the head and hump.

to form a protective shell over their coats.

Every day, all year long, bison herds graze across the prairies in a circular path, eating the grass in one area and moving on. In the 1800s, herds could be more than a thousand individuals strong and could take a full year to complete their grazing cycle. Today, with few bison and little prairie left, most herds complete their grazing cycles in a matter of days. In the winter, bison huddle together for warmth and use their massive

Bison seldom graze alone. They are gregarious animals, which means that they enjoy the company of the herd.

Bison eat only plants and grasses. Food is plentiful in summer, but in winter, bison must dig for it. Working together, a herd can dig out a 300-foot (91 m) wide path through the snow.

heads to plow through deep snow-drifts to reach food.

For most of the year, cows, calves, and young males herd together. An older cow is the leader of the herd. Older bulls tend to stay off by themselves, roaming near the herd. During **rutting season**, however, bulls join the herd to mate.

If two bulls choose the same cow, one may bellow or turn sideways in an aggressive stance, trying to frighten the other. If this doesn't work, one bull will approach the other head on, snorting and stomping its feet. One bull usually backs down, but on some occasions, a fight breaks out. Both bulls may slam their heads into each other. This usually doesn't hurt the bulls, since their skulls are thick and well-protected.

After bulls and cows mate, bison calves are born in April or early May. When it is time to give birth, the mother moves away from the herd. After the calf is born, the mother licks it clean, and the baby learns the scent and sound of its mother. A calf can stand up within minutes of birth and can run in a matter of hours. If a calf strays from its mother, the other cows in the herd help to keep it safe.

Bison have a long history on our continent. Thousands of years ago, an early type of bison lived in Asia during the **Ice Age**. These animals traveled to North America over the frozen ocean between

Newborn bison have reddish coats that darken as they age. They are not born with horns; these grow within the first year of the bison's life.

what is now Alaska and Russia. They moved further south into the United States and **evolved** into the American bison.

Native American tribes such as the Dakota, or Sioux, admired bison and relied on them in all aspects of their lives. They ate bison meat and used the hides to make clothing and homes. The bison were even part of some Native American religions. To Great Plains tribes, the bison, called *tatanka*, was awesome and powerful.

Many white settlers, however, believed that bison were in the way. In the late 1800s, the sport of bison hunting grew out of control. Railroad companies sold hunting trips. As trains passed through

Bison tear up the prairie with their strong hoofs in order to take dust baths in the dry, sun-warmed dirt.

"We were terrified at the immense numbers that were streaming down the green hills on one side of the river and galloping up over the bluffs of another."

—George Caitlin, 19th century artist, upon seeing a bison herd

herds, passengers shot their rifles through open windows. The dead bison were left on the prairie while the train moved on to the next herd. Within just a few **decades**, the great herds of bison had been nearly wiped out. Native Americans were forced to give up their lands. The population of the American bison was reduced from about 60 million animals in 1800 to less than 1,000 in 1890.

In 1894, the U.S. government made a law to save the bison. They would be protected in Yellowstone National Park. Soon, more bison were given protection. In 1904, a bison range was created in Oklahoma, and more were opened in Canada. Today, about 200,000 bison live in the United States. Some herds roam in protected public areas. Some bison ranches are privately owned.

Most herds today, whether publicly or privately managed, are fenced into certain areas. Very few herds can wander free like those in Yellowstone. Still, the number of free-roaming public herds is much larger now than it was 100 years ago. With the efforts of those who care about this powerful animal, more herds can exist in the future.

To better manage bison herds, many state and national parks sell a small number of their bison to private ranch owners each year. These people then either start or increase their own herds.

UNLIKE SOME WILD ANIMALS that are shy around humans, such as mountain lions and wolves, it is usually easy for the general public to view bison in their natural habitat. The best viewing areas are national and state parks in the western United States.

With the help of concerned people and governments, the bison is making an amazing comeback in North America. Listed here are various bison habitats with public access. As with any trek into nature, it is important to remember that wild animals are unpredictable and can be dangerous if approached. The best way to view wildlife is from a respectful—and safe—distance.

YELLOWSTONE NATIONAL PARK IN WYOMING *Yellowstone, the first area in the United States to offer protection to the bison, contains thousands of animals and numerous herds that have, for the most part, free access to roam where they choose within the park. Whether walking or driving, visitors are sure to see many bison.*

BADLANDS NATIONAL PARK IN SOUTH DAKOTA *For those who prefer to walk among wildlife, this is a spectacular viewing area. In the less-traveled south unit of the park, a bumpy dirt road leads to a primitive campground surrounded by wild prairie, dipping valleys, and limestone cliffs. There are no fences separating campers from a herd of more than 400 bison.*

WOOD BUFFALO NATIONAL PARK IN THE NORTHWEST TERRITORIES, CANADA *There are about 15,000 bison in Canada. Most of them live in this huge national park as part of the world's largest free-roaming herd. Wood Buffalo spans the Alberta-Northwest Territories border just to the south of Great Slave Lake.*

decades: *one decade equals 10 years*

evolved: *developed over a long period of time*

hindquarters: *the back legs and rear end of an animal*

Ice Age: *a prehistoric time when glaciers covered much of North America*

rutting season: *a time of the year when male animals become aggressive and prepare to mate*

vital organs: *organs that the body needs to live, such as the heart and lungs*

beard, 9
breeding, 15
calves, 9, 15
conservation, 18
ears, 9
eyes, 9
feeding, 10, 13, 15
habitat, 10, 18–19
history, 4, 10, 15, 17

horns, 6, 15
hunting, 17–18
Native Americans, 17–18
population, 18–19
predators, 9
ranches, 18, 21
running, 18
sense of smell, 9
size, 6
viewing areas, 23